THE
WEATHER
ATLAS

By Keith Lye

RUNNING PRESS
PHILADELPHIA · LONDON

Contents

 4 The air around us

 5 The atmosphere

 6 The Sun's heat

 7 The moving atmosphere

8 Winds

9 Moisture in the air

 10 Rainfall

 11 Snow, hail, and frost

 12 The water cycle

 13 Monsoons

 14 Depressions

 15 Stormy weather

16 Thunderstorms

17 Hurricanes

18 Tornadoes

19 Sandstorms and blizzards

 20 Heatwaves and floods

 21 Studying the weather

 22 Information from space

 23 Weather maps

24 Weather forecasting

25 Climate

26 Climatic regions

27 Have climates changed?

 28 Air pollution

29 Global warming

 30 Weather records

32 Index

Running Press Book Publishers
Copyright © 2001 The Ilex Press Ltd
Devised and produced by The Ilex Press Ltd, 1 West End,
Whittlesford, Cambridge

This book may not be reproduced in whole or in part in any form
or by any means, electronic or mechanical, including
photocopying, recording, or by any information storage or
retrieval system now known or hereafter invented, without written
permission from the copyright holders.

9 8 7 6 5 4 3 2 1
Digit on the right indicates the number of this printing
Library of Congress Cataloging-in-publication
number 0013 4922. ISBN 0-7624-0959-2

Art Director: Alastair Campbell
Managing Editor: Kim Yarwood
Editor: Fid Backhouse
Designer: John Carrod
Maps: Nicholas Rowland
Color separations: DPI

Published by Running Press Book Publishers
125 South Twenty-Second Street
Philadelphia, Pennsylvania 19103

Introduction

The Weather Atlas is an exciting introduction to weather and climate around the globe. Everyone is aware of the weather and we expect television, radio, or newspapers to tell us what the weather will be like in the next few hours or days. Weather forecasts help us to decide if we need coats to keep us warm or umbrellas to protect us from the rain when we leave home. In those parts of the world where severe weather conditions sometimes occur, weather warnings can save people's lives and safeguard their property.

This atlas helps to explain natural forces that create many different weather conditions. It shows why temperatures vary, why winds blow, and how clouds form. It also explains how scientists use knowledge of these natural forces to understand how weather conditions are always changing. From this knowledge, they produce the weather forecasts we take for granted.

Scientists are also interested in the climate, or weather patterns around the world. Climates have changed many times throughout Earth's history. Natural forces account for most of the changes,

The weather can be forecast by "reading" patterns in the sky.

but the activities of people have begun to affect weather and climates. Scientists are worried that air pollution is now changing world climates. Experts have confirmed that the atmosphere is getting hotter. Today, it is vital that everyone understands the reasons for weather conditions and how climatic changes could begin to affect every person in the world.

People on vacation often head for places where good weather and hot sun can be guaranteed.

Instruments like this barometer are designed to measure weather conditions. They are used by scientists, and also in the home.

Winter often brings "fairy-tale" scenery.

Our ability to monitor ever-changing weather patterns has been much improved by the use of weather satellites that look down from space.

Storms, such as tornadoes, can cause widespread damage.

The air around us

We cannot see it, smell it or taste it. But the air that surrounds us is vital for life. Without air, we would not be able to breathe in the life-giving gas, oxygen. Plants cannot survive without carbon dioxide, another gas that is a small but vital component of air.

The air also contains moisture. This occurs in the form of tiny droplets of water or ice crystals which make up clouds. But much of the moisture is in an invisible form, called water vapor. The air also contains tiny specks of volcanic ash, dust, pollen, salt, and soot.

Air has weight. This can be proved by removing air from a bottle with a vacuum pump and weighing it. The bottle with no air weighs less than the same bottle filled with air. The vast mass of air that surrounds our planet is called the atmosphere and its great weight presses down on the Earth's surface. Pressure caused by the weight of air varies. When warm air rises, air pressures fall. When cold air sinks down, air pressures start to rise.

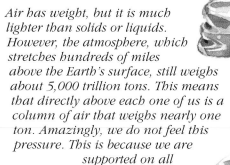

1 TON

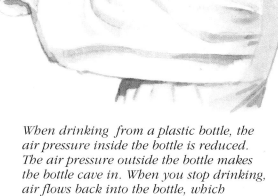

Air has weight, but it is much lighter than solids or liquids. However, the atmosphere, which stretches hundreds of miles above the Earth's surface, still weighs about 5,000 trillion tons. This means that directly above each one of us is a column of air that weighs nearly one ton. Amazingly, we do not feel this pressure. This is because we are supported on all sides by an equal pressure. In the same way, fish have adapted to survive in the great pressures that exist at the bottom of the oceans.

When drinking from a plastic bottle, the air pressure inside the bottle is reduced. The air pressure outside the bottle makes the bottle cave in. When you stop drinking, air flows back into the bottle, which resumes its normal shape.

Air contains nitrogen (78%), oxygen (21%), and argon (0.9%). There are traces of other gases, including all-important carbon dioxide (0.0335%).

Winds are currents of air which can be strong enough to push sailing boats forward at considerable speed.

High-flyers? Certain species of bird soar to heights of over 7 miles (11 km) above the Earth's surface!

Before it fades into space at an altitude of about 300 miles (480 km), the atmosphere's top three layers are: the mesosphere, the thermosphere, and the exosphere. Satellites can orbit at heights of between 155 miles (250 km) and 25,000 miles (40,000 km).

The stratosphere is above the troposphere and reaches a height of 30 miles (48 km). Manned balloons have reached the upper stratosphere.

The stratosphere's ozone layer protects people from most of the Sun's harmful ultraviolet radiation. Over-exposure to this can cause skin cancer.

Jet planes fly up to the tropopause (at the very top of the troposphere).

The troposphere is the bottom layer of the atmosphere, extending to a height of 6–10 miles (10–16 km).

Hang gliders fly comfortably at 500 feet (150 meters).

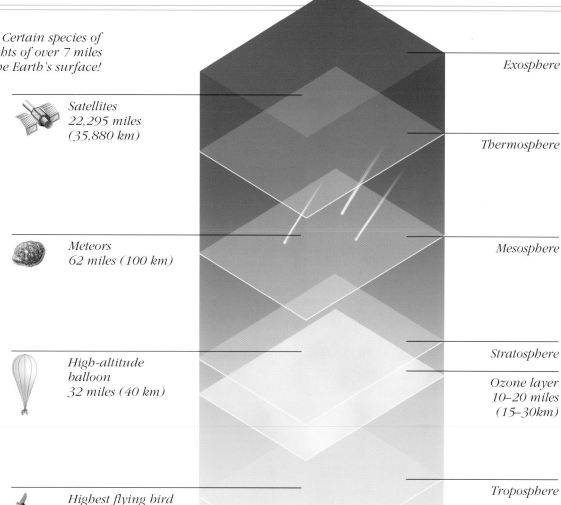

Satellites
22,295 miles
(35,880 km)

Meteors
62 miles (100 km)

High-altitude balloon
32 miles (40 km)

Highest flying bird
7 miles (11.3 km)

Jet airliners
6–10 miles
(10–16 km)

Open basket balloon
500 ft (150 m)

Hang glider
500 ft (150 m)

Exosphere

Thermosphere

Mesosphere

Stratosphere

*Ozone layer
10–20 miles
(15–30km)*

Troposphere

The atmosphere

The atmosphere is divided into five layers. The troposphere is the lowest layer. It contains four-fifths of the air in the atmosphere and most of the moisture. Almost all of the conditions we call weather occur in the troposphere.

The troposphere varies from about 6 miles (10 km) thick at the North and South Poles to 10 miles (16 km) thick at the Equator. When you fly up through the troposphere, temperatures fall by about 3.5°F for every 1,000 feet (6.5°C for every 1,000 m). Temperatures become stable at the top of the troposphere at around -67°F (-55°C). Strong winds, called jet streams, blow around the top of the troposphere and the lower stratosphere.

The stratosphere, where the air is much thinner, extends up from the troposphere to about 30 miles (48 km) above the ground. The stratosphere contains a layer of a gas called ozone.

Above the stratosphere are the mesosphere, thermosphere and exosphere. Beyond 300 miles (480 km) above the Earth, the atmosphere fades into space.

Without the atmosphere's protection, the Sun's radiation would be deadly. Even so, sun-block must be used in outdoor activities.

The Sun's heat

The Sun's rays heat the atmosphere. They also heat the land and sea areas on the Earth's surface. Warmth from the surface, in turn, heats the atmosphere.

The surface is not heated in equal amounts. Around the Equator (an imaginary line that runs around the world exactly half-way between the North and South Poles), the Sun is high in the sky. As a result, the Sun's heat is intense. But near the poles, the Sun is always low in the sky. Here, the Sun's rays pass through a greater thickness of air and are spread over a larger area of land and sea. As a result, the atmosphere is heated much less at the poles than it is at the Equator.

The amount of heating varies according to the seasons. As the Earth travels around the Sun, its axis (an imaginary line joining the North Pole, the center of the Earth, and the South Pole) is tilted. Summer in the northern half of the world occurs when the North Pole is tilted toward the Sun. Winter occurs when the northern parts of the world are tilted away from the Sun.

The world's peoples experience a variety of climates.

North Pole

Equator

South Pole

Near the North and South Poles, the Sun is low in the sky. As a result, it is very cold.

The Sun's higher position gives more warmth in those areas closer to the Equator.

On the Equator, the Sun is at its highest in the sky, so the heating effect is at its greatest.

The Sun's powerful rays heat different parts of the Earth's surface unequally.

Seasons:
As the Earth moves around the Sun, first the northern half (northern hemisphere) leans toward the Sun.
For the rest of the year, the southern hemisphere leans toward the Sun.
When your part of the Earth leans toward the Sun, it is summer.

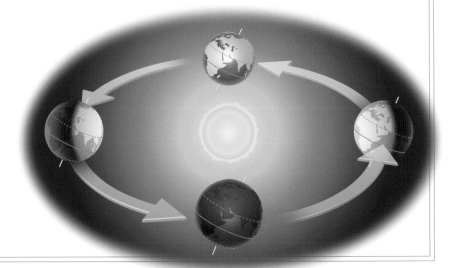

The moving atmosphere

Temperate areas are neither too hot nor too cold. They have clearly marked seasons.

Deserts occur around 30° North and 30° South of the Equator, in zones of high air pressure.

Polar regions around the North and South Poles are the coldest places on the planet.

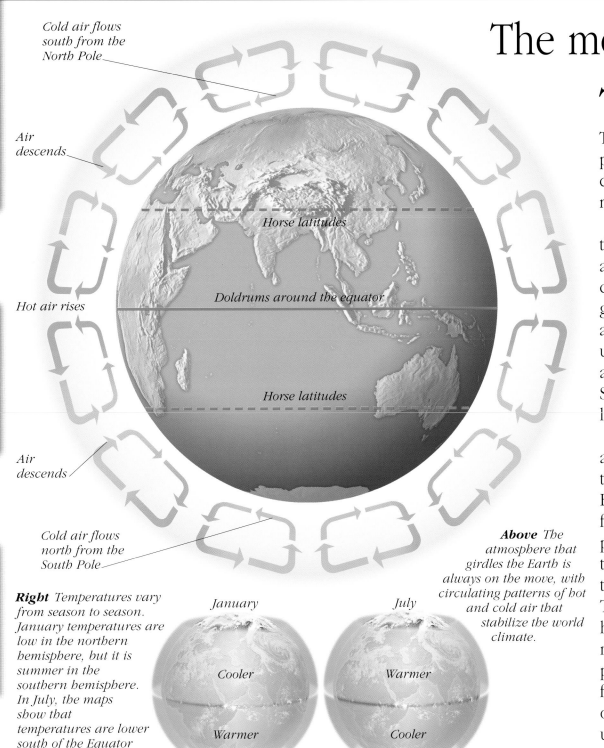

Cold air flows south from the North Pole

Air descends

Hot air rises

Air descends

Cold air flows north from the South Pole

Horse latitudes

Doldrums around the equator

Horse latitudes

Above The atmosphere that girdles the Earth is always on the move, with circulating patterns of hot and cold air that stabilize the world climate.

Right Temperatures vary from season to season. January temperatures are low in the northern hemisphere, but it is summer in the southern hemisphere. In July, the maps show that temperatures are lower south of the Equator and higher in the north.

January

Cooler

Warmer

July

Warmer

Cooler

The lines on a globe that are parallel to the Equator are called lines of latitude. The Equator is 0 degrees latitude. The two poles are 90 degrees North and 90 degrees South. Other lines of latitude are numbered between 0° and 90°.

Near the Equator, the Sun's rays heat the surface. The surface heats the air above it. Strong currents of warm air rise, creating a zone of low air pressure at ground level, called the Doldrums. As the air rises, it becomes colder. Finally, in the upper atmosphere, it spreads out north and south. Around 30° North and 30° South, the cool air sinks, creating 'horse latitudes', a zone of high air pressure.

Some descending air flows back across the surface toward the Equator and some flows towards the poles. Cold air from the poles also flows toward the Equator. These movements of hot and cold air from region to region prevent our planet from becoming overheated or unbearably cold.

Winds are light in the Doldrums, where sailing ships are often becalmed.

Winds

Winds have a great impact on weather. In the northern hemisphere, a north wind lowers temperatures, while a south wind raises them.

The main, or prevailing, winds are caused by those movements of the atmosphere described on page 7. When air sinks at the horse latitudes, around 30° North and 30° South, some air flows back toward the Equator and some flows toward the poles. The map of the world's prevailing winds shows that the air does not flow directly north or south. Instead, winds are deflected by the Earth's rotation—to the right of the direction in which they naturally flow in the northern hemisphere and to the left in the southern hemisphere. The winds blowing from the horse latitudes toward the Doldrums are called trade winds. The winds blowing from the horse latitudes toward the poles are called westerly winds. Cold winds blowing from the poles toward the Equator are called polar easterlies.

Left The combination of strong winds and high tides can flood coastal areas.

Using the wind to make a kite fly high can be fun—but wind also plays a vital role in shaping the world's weather.

The map below shows the neat pattern of the world's prevailing winds.

Maritime polar air mass

Continental polar air mass

Cold winds blow south

Maritime polar air mass

Maritime polar air mass

Maritime tropical air mass

Continental tropical air mass

Maritime tropical air mass

Polar easterlies

Westerlies

30° North

Northeast trade winds

Equator

Southeast trade winds

30° South

Westerlies

Polar easterlies

Above The map shows a good example of how winds help to determine climate. In winter, winds blow from cold air masses that form over the northern part of North America, to meet warmer winds coming up from the Equator. These stop the cold air from reaching the southern part of the United States, which never experiences the bitterly cold winters of the northern part. In between, the winter weather rarely reaches either extreme.

Cool breezes blow from the colder sea to the warmer land by day.

At night the process is reversed, with breezes blowing off cooling land toward the warmer sea.

Moisture in the air

If you leave a saucer of water outside in warm weather, the water eventually disappears. The Sun's heat has turned the water into invisible water vapor. This process is called evaporation, a term used by scientists for changes that take place when a liquid or solid is converted into a gas or turned into a vapor.

Warm air can hold more water vapor than cold air. But, as the air cools, its capacity to hold water vapor is reduced. Cooling air eventually reaches a point when it is saturated—that is, it contains all the water vapor it can hold at that temperature. This is called the dew point. Further cooling means that the air starts to lose water vapor. The invisible vapor then turns back into visible water droplets or tiny ice crystals.

Clouds are formed in this way. When warm air rises from the ground, it gradually becomes cooled. Eventually, tiny droplets of water, or ice crystals, start to form around specks or other matter in the air. This process is called condensation. Clouds are formed from billions of water droplets or ice crystals.

On cold days, warm breath turns into a cloud of water vapor.

Condensation occurs when water vapor turns into water droplets. For example, droplets form when warm air comes into contact with a cold window pane. Dew is similar. It forms in the early morning when beads of water form on plants and leaves.

Clouds are classified according to their height above the ground.
Clouds above 20,000 ft (6,100 m) are called high clouds and include cirrus, cirrostratus and cirrocumulus.
Medium clouds, at 8,200 ft (2,500 m), include altocumulus and altostratus.
Nimbostratus, stratocumulus, cumulus and stratus are all low clouds.
Cumulonimbus (thunder clouds) start as low clouds, but they may grow into large, high clouds.

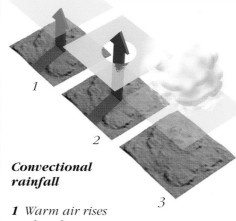

A
B
C
D
E
F
G
H
I
J

A
Cirrus

B
Cirrostratus

C
Cirrocumulus

D
Altocumulus

E
Altostratus

F
Cumulonimbus

G
Nimbostratus

H
Stratocumulus

I
Cumulus

J
Stratus

Convectional rainfall

1 Warm air rises and cools.

2 As the air cools, the invisible vapor condenses.

3 Cumulus clouds form.

Rainfall

When clouds form, the water droplets are too light to fall to the ground. But when they collide inside clouds, they grow until they are heavy enough to form raindrops. Rain may also form from ice crystals. Ice crystals grow as cold droplets freeze around them. As they fall, ice crystals can melt and become raindrops.

Rain is formed in several ways. On warm days, the Sun evaporates moisture which is swept upwards by currents of warm air. As the air cools, clouds form and rain falls. This is called convectional rain. When wind from the sea passes over mountains, the air rises and cools. Clouds form and rain falls on the mountain slopes. This is called orographic rain.

Above Rainbows are formed when the Sun's rays pass through droplets of water which split white light into the colors of the rainbow.

Above Heavy or prolonged rainfall sometimes causes floods, which can wash away buildings and cars. Disastrous floods can cause great loss of human life.

Above Annual rainfall varies greatly around the world. Some areas are deserts, while others have so much rainfall that floods are common. Dark blue areas have over 80 in (2,030 mm) of rain; light blue, 20–40 in (500–1,000 mm). Green areas have 10–20 in (250–500 mm) of rain and yellow areas have under 10 in (250 mm) a year.

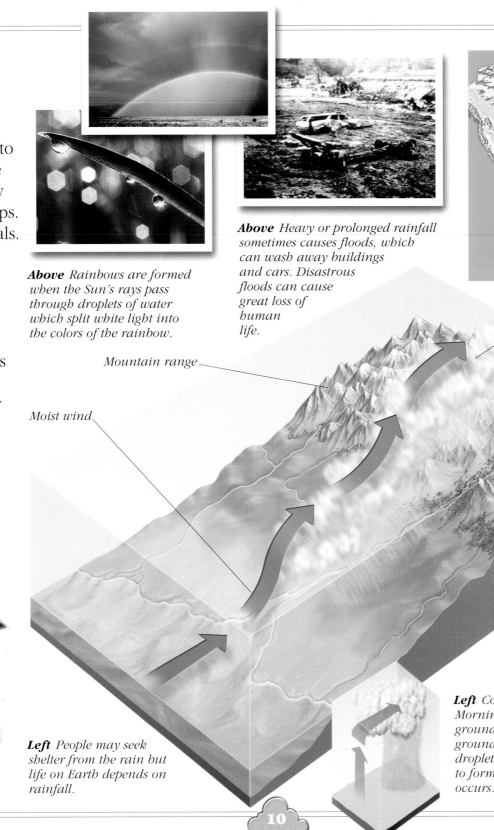

Clouds form

Mountain range

Moist wind

Left Orographic rain occurs when moist winds from the sea cross over mountain ranges. The rising air is cooled, clouds form, and heavy rain or snow falls on the mountain slopes. Once they pass the crest of mountain ranges, the winds start to descend. The air then becomes warmer and moisture is evaporated. The leeward sides of ranges are therefore said to be in a rain shadow area which is dry.

Left Convectional rainfall is common near the Equator. Morning skies are often clear. Then intense heating of the ground causes warm, moist air to rise. High above the ground, the air cools and water vapor condenses into water droplets, forming massive thunderclouds. The droplets fuse to form raindrops and, in the late afternoon, heavy rain occurs. After the storm, the sky clears.

Left People may seek shelter from the rain but life on Earth depends on rainfall.

Above *Hailstorms often cause great damage, as large hailstones are capable of denting cars.*

Above *Playing in the snow is fun, but snow can also cause transport problems.*

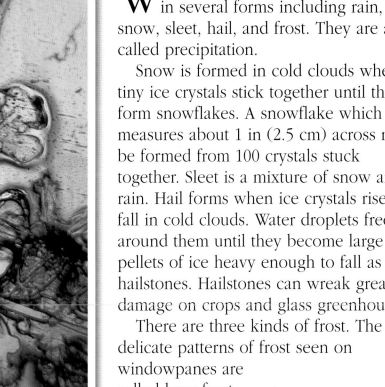

Above *A snowflake, shown here magnified under a microscope, is formed from around 100 ice crystals that are stuck together.*

Above *The combination of snow, ice, and frost turns the countryside into a winter wonderland.*

Left *Beautiful fern-like patterns of frost are made up of frozen water droplets, often appearing on windows in icy weather.*

Water reaches the ground from the air in several forms including rain, snow, sleet, hail, and frost. They are all called precipitation.

Snow is formed in cold clouds when tiny ice crystals stick together until they form snowflakes. A snowflake which measures about 1 in (2.5 cm) across may be formed from 100 crystals stuck together. Sleet is a mixture of snow and rain. Hail forms when ice crystals rise and fall in cold clouds. Water droplets freeze around them until they become large pellets of ice heavy enough to fall as hailstones. Hailstones can wreak great damage on crops and glass greenhouses.

There are three kinds of frost. The delicate patterns of frost seen on windowpanes are called hoar frost. Thick coatings of ice which form on cold surfaces are called glazed frost. The third kind of frost, rime, forms when extremely cold water droplets freeze on contact with cold surfaces.

4 in (100 mm) of snow is almost the same as 0.4 in (10 mm) of rainfall.

The water cycle

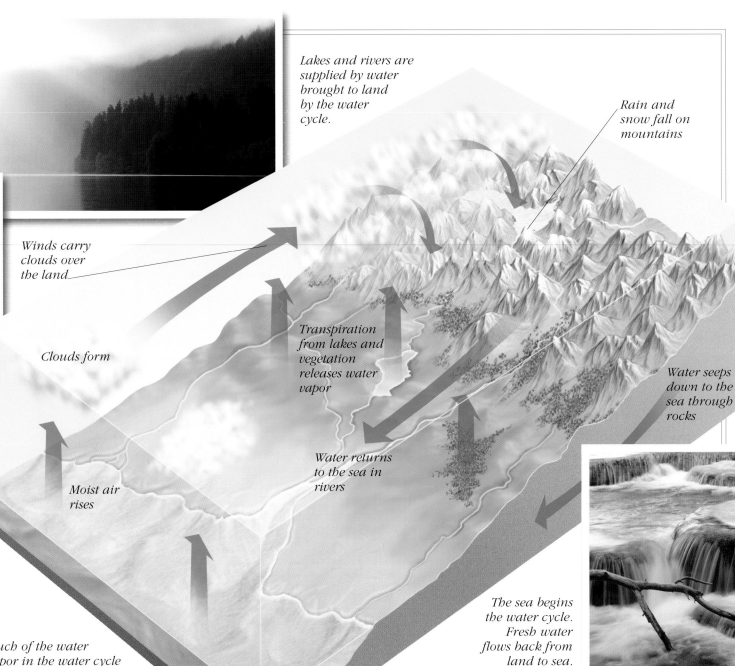

About 97% of the world's water is in the oceans. Sea water is far too salty for drinking or farming. But a natural process called the water cycle ensures that the land gets a regular supply of essential fresh water.

The cycle begins when the Sun evaporates water from the sea. Water vapor, which makes up only 0.001% of the world's water, is swept into the air where it condenses to form clouds. Winds blow the clouds over the land. Rain from clouds runs into rivers and sinks into the ground. In mountains, snow falls. But this snow eventually melts and adds to the fresh water supply.

Gravity ensures that most of the water that reaches land eventually finds its way back into the oceans, and the water cycle is completed.

The Sun makes water evaporate from both land and sea to form rain-bearing clouds.

Trees and plants cannot survive without fresh water from the water cycle.

Much of the water vapor in the water cycle comes from the oceans. Water also evaporates from rivers and lakes, and water vapor is released by plants through their leaves—a process called transpiration. Gravity ensures that most of the water from land areas makes its way back to the sea, where the cycle begins again.

Lakes and rivers are supplied by water brought to land by the water cycle.

Rain and snow fall on mountains

Winds carry clouds over the land

Clouds form

Transpiration from lakes and vegetation releases water vapor

Water seeps down to the sea through rocks

Moist air rises

Water returns to the sea in rivers

The sea begins the water cycle. Fresh water flows back from land to sea.

Monsoons

Four main factors—temperature, wind, moisture, and air pressure—affect weather conditions in the troposphere. Changes in air pressure cause monsoons (seasonal reversals of wind directions). The best-known monsoon occurs in the Indian subcontinent.

In winter, the land in southern Asia is chilled and cool air sinks, creating a high pressure air mass. Northeasterly winds blow outwards from this mass. In spring, the land warms and hot air rises, creating a low pressure air mass. Southwesterly winds laden with water vapor from the oceans are then drawn into southern Asia. Summer winds formed in this way bring abundant rain to southern and southeastern Asia—rain vital to farmers who depend on it for their crops. But if the rains are too heavy, they can destroy crops and cause floods that drown people and animals.

Other monsoons occur in eastern Asia, northern Australia, parts of Africa, and the southwestern United States.

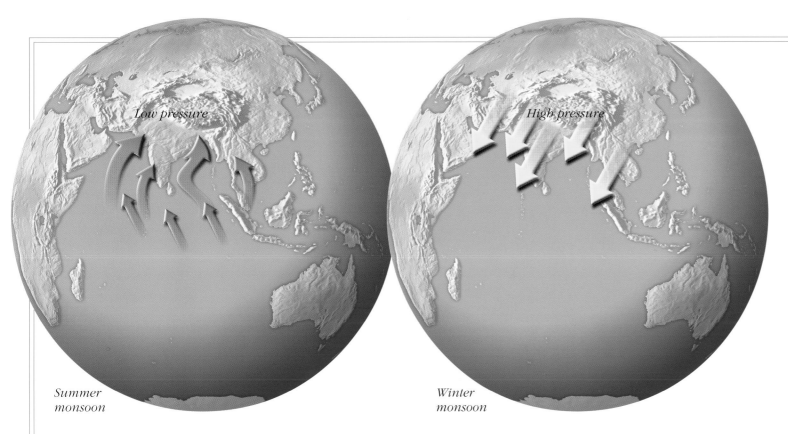

Low pressure

Summer monsoon

High pressure

Winter monsoon

Above *The maps show how wind directions in southern Asia are reversed between summer and winter. The summer winds (left) come from the sea and bring huge amounts of water to the land. In winter, dry winds blow off the land.*

Below *Trees cannot grow unless there is water in the soil which the plants can absorb through their roots.*

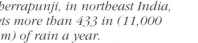

Above *Monsoon regions with wet summer winds get heavy rainfall and floods.*

Cherrapunji, in northeast India, gets more than 433 in (11,000 mm) of rain a year.

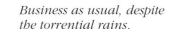

Business as usual, despite the torrential rains.

Sheltering from a sudden downpour!

Depressions

In some parts of the world, the weather is stable. In other places, it can often change from hour to hour. Changeable weather is caused by low air pressure systems, which are called depressions or cyclones. By contrast, high pressure anticyclones usually bring stable weather.

Depressions are circular air systems. They form along the polar front, where warm westerly winds meet up with cold, dense air flowing from the poles. Warm and cold air do not mix easily. When warm air flows into waves in the polar front, it flows over the cold air. Cold air then follows along behind the warm air and a depression is born.

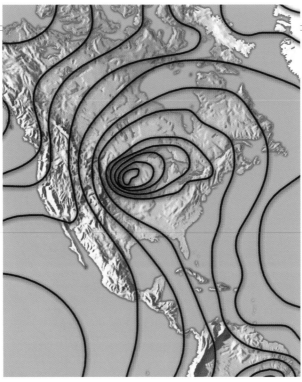

Above On weather maps the circular lines, also called isobars, surround areas with equal air pressure. Depressions can be recognized because the lowest value of air pressure is found at their center.

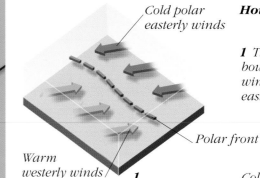

Cold polar easterly winds

Warm westerly winds

Polar front

1

How depressions form:

1 The polar front is the boundary where warm westerly winds meet up with cold polar easterly winds.

2 Waves develop in the polar front. Warm air flows into these waves, forming two fronts. Cold fronts are shown by lines marked with tiny triangles. Warm fronts are shown as lines with semi-circles along them.

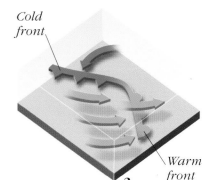

Cold front

Warm front

2

3 A fully formed depression consists of dense cold air, with light warm air at the center. The cold air undercuts the warm air along the front. Along the warm front, the warm air flows above the cold air.

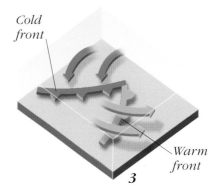

Cold front

Warm front

3

4 The cold air eventually catches up with the warm front, forming an occlusion. An occlusion is shown by a line with alternating triangles and semi-circles.

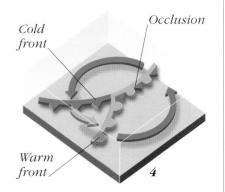

Cold front

Occlusion

Warm front

4

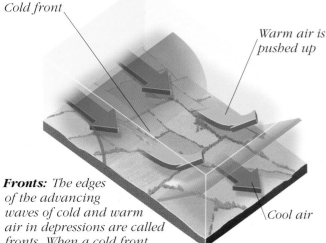

Cold front

Warm air is pushed up

Cool air

Fronts: The edges of the advancing waves of cold and warm air in depressions are called fronts. When a cold front catches up with a warm front and overtakes it, the warm air is pushed above the cold air. This is called an occluded front. Cold fronts often move at twice the speed of the warm fronts they are chasing.

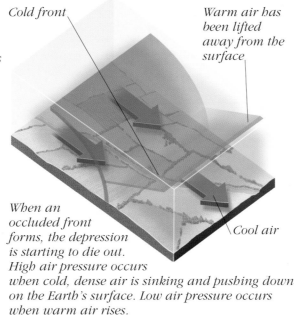

Cold front

Warm air has been lifted away from the surface

Cool air

When an occluded front forms, the depression is starting to die out. High air pressure occurs when cold, dense air is sinking and pushing down on the Earth's surface. Low air pressure occurs when warm air rises.

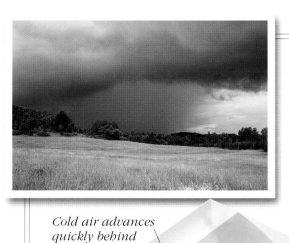

Stormy weather and thunderstorms are features of cold and warm fronts.

Above Rain falling from banks of clouds that accompany fronts.

Left Storm clouds tower into the sky.

Cold air advances quickly behind the warm air.

Cold front

After the warm front has passed, the skies clear.

Warm air rises over the cold air along the warm front.

Warm front

Cool air

Clouds form and rain falls ahead of the warm front.

This diagram shows a depression, or 'low', passing over the land. It consists of a wedge of warm, rising air between areas of cold, sinking air. Storms often occur at the meeting points of warm and cold fronts. Depressions are rotating storms that occur in temperate regions. They measure 100–1,860 miles (160–3,000 km) across. In the northern hemisphere, winds rotate around depressions in an anti-clockwise direction. In the southern hemisphere, the winds rotate in a clockwise direction.

Light rain or snow are the main weather features when an occlusion passes overhead.

Stormy weather

Stormy and changeable weather is the main feature of depressions. Ahead of the warm front, clouds form as warm, light air flows above the cold air ahead of it. The first clouds that appear when a warm front is advancing are high cirrus clouds. Later, the clouds are lower. They bring light but persistent rain or snow.

After the warm front has passed, temperatures increase and skies clear. But soon the cold front arrives. It travels about twice as fast as the warm front. When it arrives, temperatures fall. Cold air forms a wedge beneath the warm air, forcing it upwards. If the warm air contains a lot of water vapor, huge thunderclouds called cumulonimbus may form in the rising air along the cold front. But stormy weather and heavy rain or snow from these clouds do not last for long.

When a cold front catches up with a warm front, an occluded front is formed. Along an occluded front, warm air is pushed above cold air. Clouds continue to form and rain and snow still fall. But the weather along an occluded front is less extreme and long-lasting than along warm and cold fronts.

The calm before the storm.

Thunderstorms

On average, 45,000 thunderstorms occur around the world every day. Many of these happen in regions near the Equator, where strong currents of moist air rise upwards. Water vapor condenses to form cumulonimbus clouds. These are the breeding ground for lightning and thunder. Cumulonimbus clouds occur in temperate regions, on hot summer days or along cold fronts.

Lightning, which can start fires and kill people, is made up of huge electrical sparks. It occurs one or more strokes. The forked lightning that follows a jagged path across the sky is called a return stroke. Return strokes travel at the speed of light, which is 186,282 miles/sec (299,792 km/sec).

Forked lightning strikes.

Cumulonimbus clouds are an ominous sight.

*The sequence above shows one theory on why lightning occurs. The center of hailstones in clouds have a negative charge, while the outside is positively charged (**1**). When the hailstones break up, positive light outer fragments are swept up (**2**) while heavy negative cores fall to the base of the cloud (**3**). The charges are discharged as a huge electric spark (**4**). Lightning may be attracted from the cloud base to positively charged high buildings or the ground (**5**), and the return stroke generates further strikes (**6**).*

Cumulonimbus clouds form

Warm, moist air rises

Above *Cumulonimbus clouds, which cause thunderstorms, form when warm, moist air rises. Lightning, which occurs in these clouds, heats up the air along its path. The hot air particles collide with cooler air, creating thunder. We see lightning before we hear thunder because light travels faster than sound. A thunderstorm does not always produce visible lightning.*

Hurricanes

Thunderstorms are the most common storms, but hurricanes are the most destructive. Hurricanes batter Caribbean islands, Central America, and the eastern coasts of the United States. Hurricanes in eastern Asia are called typhoons. In southern Asia they are known as tropical cyclones, while in Australia they are called willy-willies.

Hurricanes develop in the trade wind belt north and south of the Equator. They have a core, or eye, where pressure is low. Around the eye, warm air rises to create storm clouds and violent winds that rotate at up to 186 mph (300 km/h).

Hurricanes are much larger than thunderstorms, often measuring 120–310 miles (200–500 km) across. When they reach land, huge waves crash against the shore and cause serious flooding.

Above Hurricane-force winds can reach speeds of up to 186 mph (300 km/h).

Above Photographed from space, the eye at the center of a hurricane is clearly visible. A period of calm occurs when the eye passes over, but following the eye comes a second violent onslaught.

Above Hurricanes are capable of awesome destruction when they reach land.

Hurricanes have a central eye around which are huge circular bands of cumulus and cumulonimbus clouds. The top clouds are made of ice, but lower clouds are composed of water droplets. The hurricane is powered by fast-rotating winds. Hurricanes form over the oceans. On average, 11 reach North America's shores every year. They bring fierce winds and torrential rain, but soon die out over the mainland.

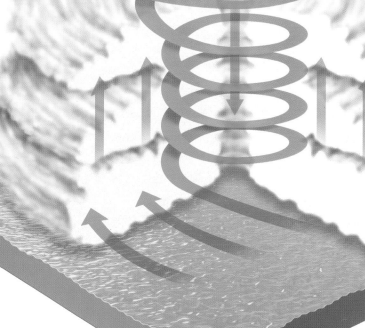

It's hard to walk when hurricane winds blow.

Tornadoes

The most violent storms that form over land areas are called tornadoes. They are small weather systems, measuring only about 0.25 miles (0.4 km) across at ground level, but they can cause great destruction.

Also called 'twisters', tornadoes form when rotating funnels of cloud sink down from cumulonimbus clouds, as warm air rises and rotates around the funnel. Some funnels do not reach the ground. Some reach the ground, withdraw, and then come down again. Tornadoes are short-lived. Most of them last no more than an hour.

Air pressures are extremely low in the center of the tornadoes. The difference in air pressure in a tornado and the inside of a building can make the building explode. Tornadoes also tear trees out of the ground and lift cars and people into the air. When tornadoes develop over water, they form features called waterspouts.

The United States is hit by around 600 to 700 tornadoes a year, mostly in spring and early summer.

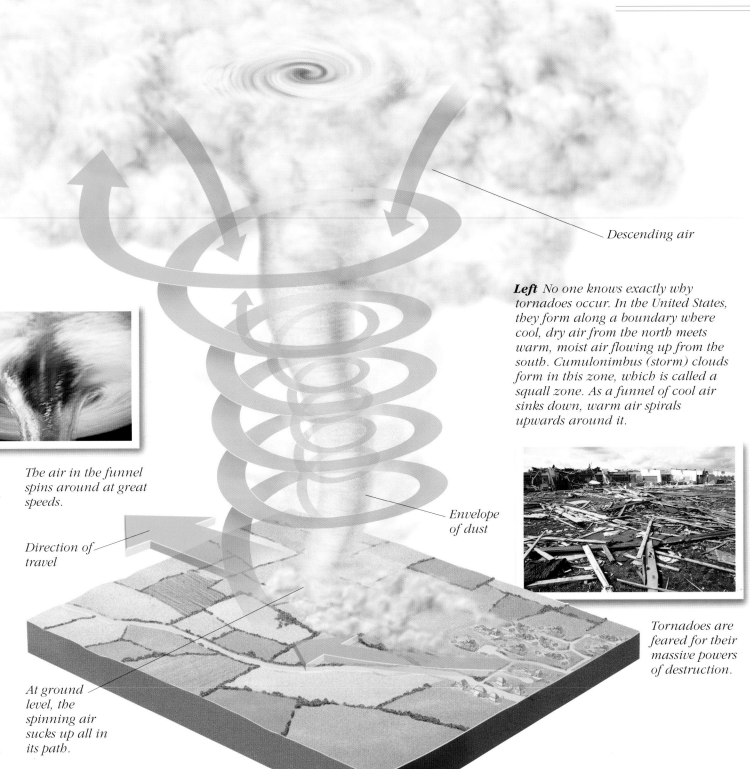

The air in the funnel spins around at great speeds.

Direction of travel

At ground level, the spinning air sucks up all in its path.

Descending air

Left *No one knows exactly why tornadoes occur. In the United States, they form along a boundary where cool, dry air from the north meets warm, moist air flowing up from the south. Cumulonimbus (storm) clouds form in this zone, which is called a squall zone. As a funnel of cool air sinks down, warm air spirals upwards around it.*

Envelope of dust

Tornadoes are feared for their massive powers of destruction.

Tornadoes are frequent in the central and southern United States.

Sandstorms and blizzards

Sandstorms and duststorms occur in deserts. During sandstorms, the wind lifts up grains of sand and bounces them across the surface. Sand grains are heavy, and they are seldom lifted more than 6.6 ft (2 m). But sandstorms are very unpleasant. Wind-blown sand affects desert scenery, because it acts like a natural sandblaster. Duststorms can be dangerous to aircraft because clouds of dust can be lifted to heights of 9,840 ft (3,000 m) or more.

Blinding blizzards occur in polar regions and also in temperate areas affected by cold Arctic air masses.

They are caused by strong, bitterly cold winds that whip up dry, powdery snow and ice from the surface. Wind speeds in blizzards reach 35–45 mph (56–72 km/h). They occur in northern North America and Russia.

North America and Siberia are also hit by icestorms. They happen when rain or wet (melting) snow freezes onto cold surfaces, such as roads or vehicles.

Above *Wind-blown sand shapes the scenery in deserts. Unless they are protected by metal, sand can cut down wooden telegraph poles, strip paint from cars, hollow out caves, and undercut boulders. Over countless years, sand has shaped desert landscape by sculpting all sorts of weird and wonderful rock formations.*

Left *Severe blizzards can cause serious disruption, even in cities. They can stop all traffic and cause businesses to close down.*

Above *Wind-blown sand during sandstorms can be very painful, but usually the heads of adults remain above the level of swirling sand grains. Choking dust clouds, however, can be lifted to much greater heights* (**above right**).

Right *The hardy people who live near the poles are used to surviving in blizzard conditions.*

Desert peoples are always ready to protect themselves from sandstorms.

Heatwaves and floods

Besides storms, other unusual weather conditions can also cause damage and loss of life. For example, some areas experience periods when temperatures soar way above the average. People feel uncomfortable, especially if the amount of water vapor in the air (humidity) is high. Heat can also lead to deaths—in 1980 an estimated 1,500 people died during a heatwave in the United States.

Periods of great heat are often accompanied by drought, when no rain falls for weeks or months. Droughts dry up the land and the plants on it. Dry plants burn easily, often causing forest fires. In Africa, long droughts kill the animals of nomadic herders, who then starve.

When droughts occur, people pray for rain. But too much rain can swell rivers until they overflow, causing terrible floods that destroy people and property. In Africa and Asia, after floods subside, people are at risk from diseases like cholera and malaria.

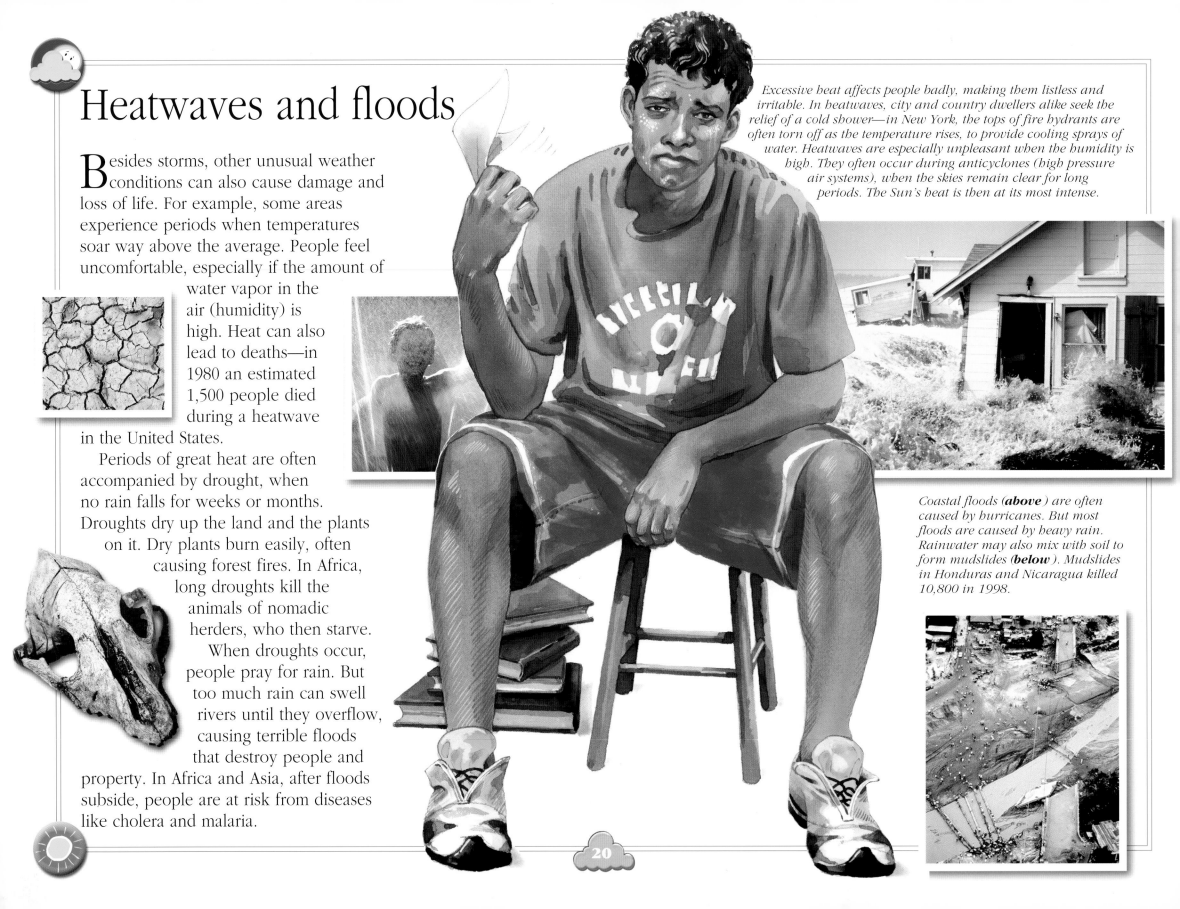

Excessive heat affects people badly, making them listless and irritable. In heatwaves, city and country dwellers alike seek the relief of a cold shower—in New York, the tops of fire hydrants are often torn off as the temperature rises, to provide cooling sprays of water. Heatwaves are especially unpleasant when the humidity is high. They often occur during anticyclones (high pressure air systems), when the skies remain clear for long periods. The Sun's heat is then at its most intense.

*Coastal floods (**above**) are often caused by hurricanes. But most floods are caused by heavy rain. Rainwater may also mix with soil to form mudslides (**below**). Mudslides in Honduras and Nicaragua killed 10,800 in 1998.*

Studying the weather

Right *Aneroid barometers show changes in air pressure. Falling pressure often means that rain is on the way.*

Left *A sunshine recorder enables statistics to be kept on the the hours when the Sun shines.*

Above *A barograph uses a pen that records changing air pressures on a paper chart mounted on a rotating drum.*

The weather affects our lives in many ways. It determines the clothes we wear when we go out. Weather is also important to farmers and to people working in communications, industry, and transport. For example, a sudden frost or hailstorm can severely damage a farmer's crops, while icy roads are a hazard for truck drivers. The science of weather is called meteorology and the people who study it are meteorologists. Many of them work in weather forecasting.

Fir cones react to humidity. When the air is dry, the cone closes up. When it is humid, the cone quickly opens up.

To produce a forecast, different elements of weather must be measured. These include temperature, air pressures, wind speeds and directions, and rainfall. Around the world, meteorologists at weather stations on land or on ships at sea measure weather conditions.

Meteorologists collect and analyze information from weather stations. They must interpret all the complex information before predicting how weather patterns are likely to develop.

Above *Thermometers are used to measure temperature. To avoid exposure to direct sunlight and record the correct air temperature, they are kept in shelters.*

Hi-tech sensors (**above**) measure wind speed by its sound. Cup anemometers (**below**) rotate as the wind blows and record wind speeds. Vanes indicate wind direction.

Above *A rain gauge measures rainfall. The inside is shaped like a funnel, with a tube to hold the water.*

CASELLA

Cows can give clues about the weather— when they lie down, it may indicate storms are on the way.

Information from space

The accuracy of weather forecasts has increased greatly in the past 50 years, because we now know much more about conditions in the upper atmosphere.

A major breakthrough came with the use of radio-sondes. A radio-sonde is a large hydrogen-filled balloon that carries instruments to measure temperatures and air pressures, with a radio to transmit the data back to the ground. When the balloon bursts at high altitude, the instrument pack floats down attached to a parachute.

A weather satellite.

Other information comes from weather satellites, which photograph cloud patterns over the Earth. They also measure the temperature and humidity in the upper atmosphere. Jet aircraft send back information about weather conditions in the upper troposphere and lower stratosphere, while radar locates bands of rain.

Left Some weather satellites are launched into space by rocket, while others are deployed by the USA's space shuttle.

Above *Television cameras in satellites send back pictures of the Earth and its weather to ground stations. These pictures are analyzed to provide weather forecasters with information that can be captured in no other way. Some weather satellites circle the Earth from pole to pole. Others are positioned over the Equator to move around in unison with the rotating Earth.*

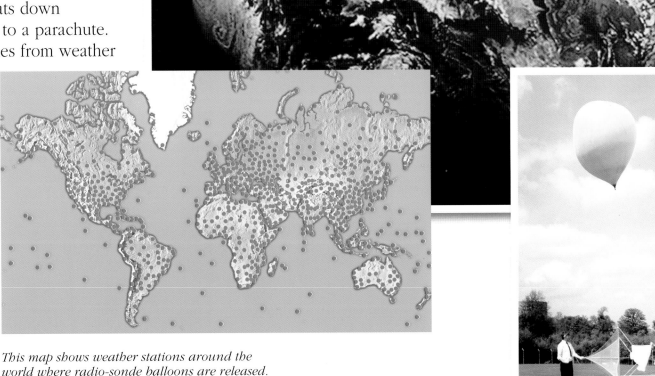

This map shows weather stations around the world where radio-sonde balloons are released.

Left *Weather balloons carry radio-sondes high into the upper atmosphere.*

Hundreds of weather stations around the world gather the information needed for accurate weather maps.

Warm fronts are identified on weather maps by orange semi-circles. Cold fronts are identified by blue triangles.

Occluded fronts can include both warm (orange) and blue (cold) air.

Weather maps

At more than 7,000 weather stations around the world, meteorologists measure conditions in the air at ground level and often at various layers in the upper atmosphere. At some stations, they record information every 30 minutes. Other stations make measurements every 6 or 12 hours. Stations transmit this information to weather centers, where it is fed into computers that prepare weather maps.

Weather maps prepared by computers are called synoptic charts, because they give a "synopsis", or summary, of weather conditions on the ground and at various levels in the atmosphere at a point in time.

These weather maps show isobars, which are circular lines indicating the positions of depressions and anticyclones. Other features can then be added to the maps, including temperatures, wind speeds and directions, precipitation, and cloud cover. The synoptic charts provide all the information that is needed for meteorologists to prepare the most accurate weather forecasts possible.

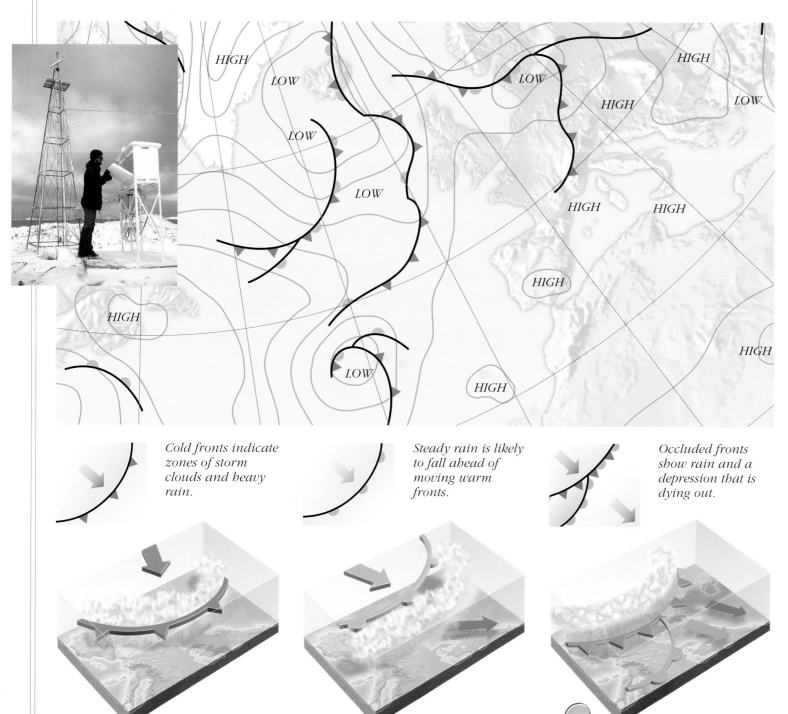

Cold fronts indicate zones of storm clouds and heavy rain.

Steady rain is likely to fall ahead of moving warm fronts.

Occluded fronts show rain and a depression that is dying out.

A vast array of data is used to predict changing weather patterns.

Weather forecasting

Synoptic charts show how the weather has changed over the past few days. Armed with this knowledge, meteorologists produce prognostic charts. They give a prognosis (or forecast) of what the weather will be like in 24, 36, or 48 hours' time. From these charts, meteorologists supply written forecasts to newspapers, radio, and TV stations. Some forecasts are short-range, covering the next 24–36 hours, while extended or long-range forecasts cover five days or more.

Computers are almost always used to produce forecasts. But meteorologists still have an important role to play. Often, they have recent information not available to the computer. They also have the experience to allow for local factors. Forecasting today involves an effective collaboration between skilled people and computers. Short-range forecasts now reach a high level of accuracy. But for all the sophisticated technology available to forecasters, mistakes do occur. For example, a storm may start in an area where there are few stations.

Tomorrow

Left Weather maps on TV often use neat symbols that do not appear on prognostic charts. TV forecast maps are simplified to make them easy to understand at a glance.

Aircraft play a vital part in gathering information— with both special weather planes and commercial flights reporting data.

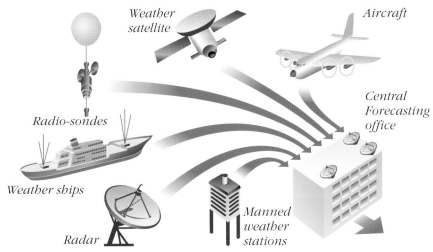

Weather satellite

Aircraft

Radio-sondes

Central Forecasting office

Weather ships

Manned weather stations

Radar

***Above** Information reaches the weather center from a vast number of sources. This is used to produce forecasts that are supplied to airports,* the media, farmers, sailors, and many others affected by the weather.

***Above** The importance of accurate forecasts to the modern world can be judged by the vast technical and human* resources put into today's weather centers.

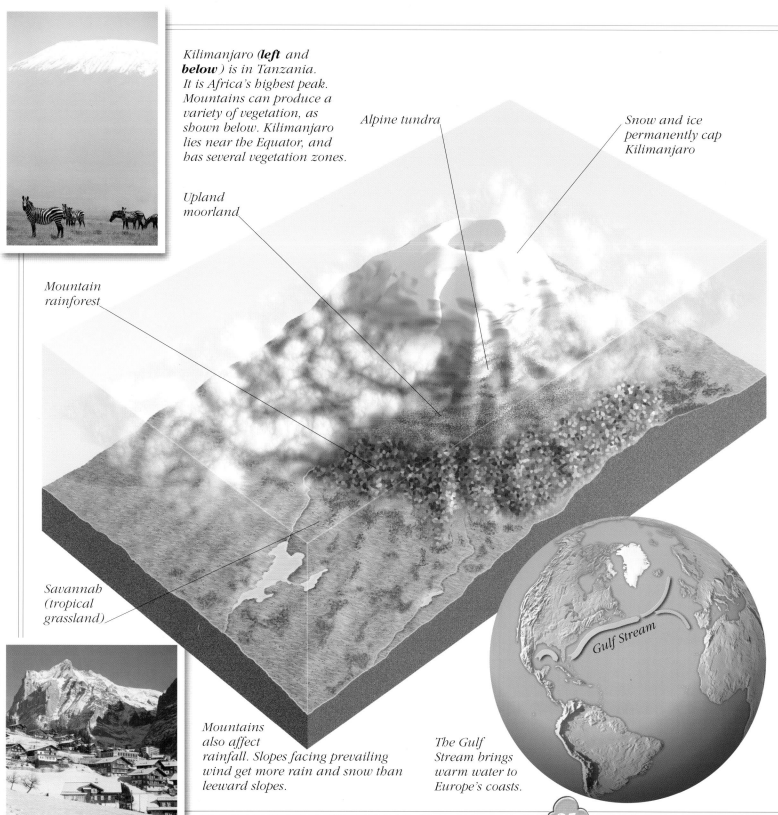

*Kilimanjaro (**left** and **below**) is in Tanzania. It is Africa's highest peak. Mountains can produce a variety of vegetation, as shown below. Kilimanjaro lies near the Equator, and has several vegetation zones.*

Alpine tundra

Snow and ice permanently cap Kilimanjaro

Upland moorland

Mountain rainforest

Savannah (tropical grassland)

Mountains also affect rainfall. Slopes facing prevailing wind get more rain and snow than leeward slopes.

The Gulf Stream brings warm water to Europe's coasts.

Gulf Stream

Climate

Weather is the hour-to-hour state of the atmosphere, while climate is the usual, or average, weather of a place. Several factors influence climate. One is latitude, or how close you are to the Equator or to the poles.

Other factors are important. Because temperatures fall with height, by 1°F for every 300 ft (7°C for every 1,000 m), mountain tops on the Equator are cold. Mountains also affect rainfall. Slopes facing the wind (windward) are rainier than those sheltered from the wind (leeward).

Climate is also affected by the sea and ocean currents. A warm current called the Gulf Stream flows from the hot Caribbean Sea region to northwestern Europe. Winds that blow on to the shore across this warm current bring mild weather to some regions that would otherwise be much colder. The farther you go from the sea, the more extreme is the climate. In the heart of a continent, summers are normally hotter and winters colder than in coastal regions.

The Gulf Stream warms the climate on the west coasts of northwest Europe. This allows semi-tropical plants to grow in places where it should be too cold for them to survive.

Climatic regions

There are six main kinds of climate. Polar climates include areas covered by snow and ice. Treeless areas, called tundra, have a short summer when the snow melts and plants grow. Polar regions have little rain or snow.

Cold snowy climates have long winters. Forests of coniferous trees (trees with cones and, usually, hard, needle-like leaves) grow in this climate. Coniferous trees include fir and pine.

Mid-latitude or temperate climates have warm summers and cold to mild winters. Typical trees growing in this climatic zone include ash, beech, and oak. They shed leaves in fall and grow new ones in spring.

Dry climates are places where average annual rainfall is less than 10 in (250 mm). They include deserts and dry grasslands, such as the prairies of North America.

Tropical rainy climates are hot and wet. Dense rainforests grow in places with rain throughout the year. Other areas are wet but they have a marked dry season. Such areas are often covered by savannah, or tropical grassland with scattered trees.

High mountains contain different zones of climates. Near the Equator, rainforests or savanna may flourish at the base, with polar conditions where nothing grows at the very top.

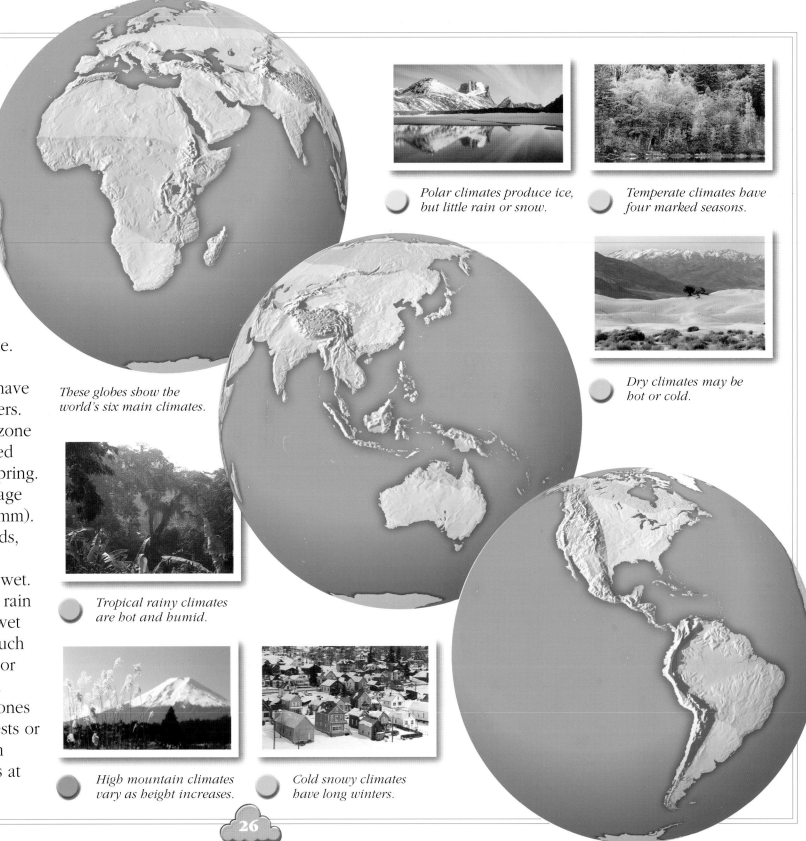

These globes show the world's six main climates.

Polar climates produce ice, but little rain or snow.

Temperate climates have four marked seasons.

Dry climates may be hot or cold.

Tropical rainy climates are hot and humid.

High mountain climates vary as height increases.

Cold snowy climates have long winters.

Have climates changed?

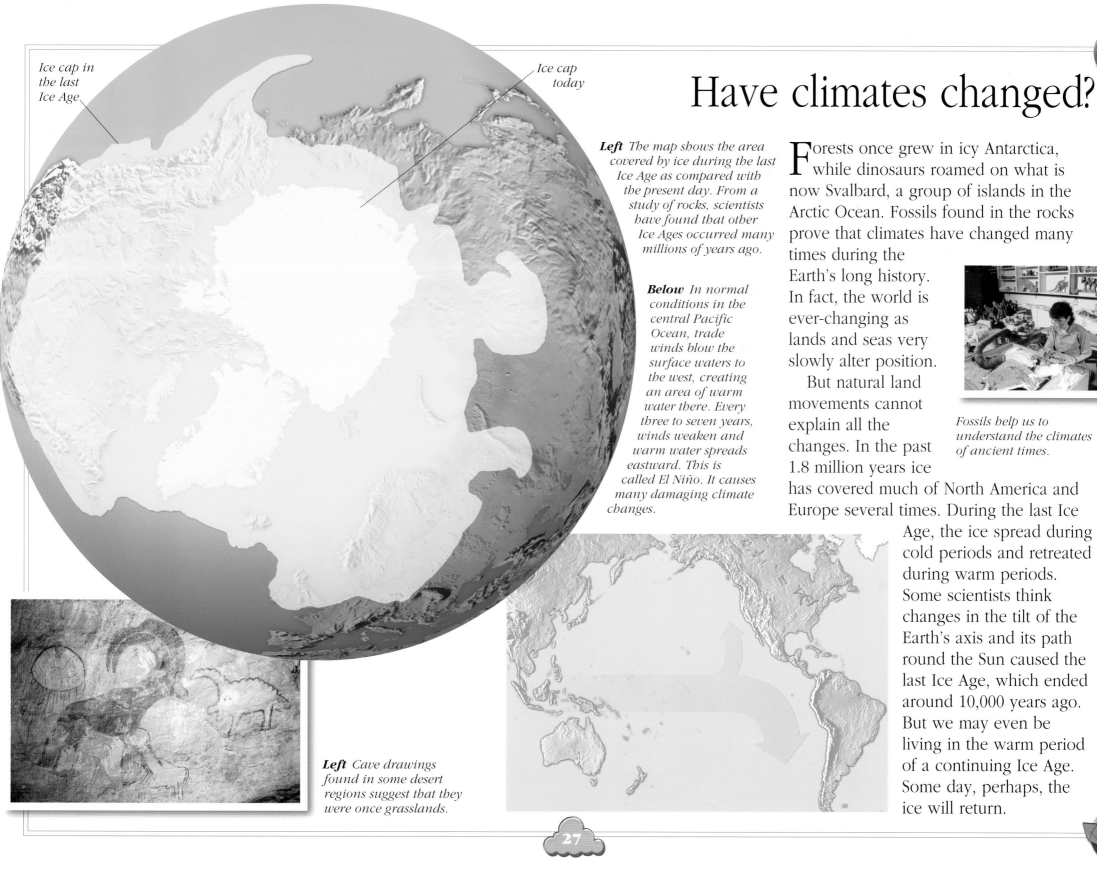

Ice cap in the last Ice Age

Ice cap today

Left *The map shows the area covered by ice during the last Ice Age as compared with the present day. From a study of rocks, scientists have found that other Ice Ages occurred many millions of years ago.*

Below *In normal conditions in the central Pacific Ocean, trade winds blow the surface waters to the west, creating an area of warm water there. Every three to seven years, winds weaken and warm water spreads eastward. This is called El Niño. It causes many damaging climate changes.*

Left *Cave drawings found in some desert regions suggest that they were once grasslands.*

Forests once grew in icy Antarctica, while dinosaurs roamed on what is now Svalbard, a group of islands in the Arctic Ocean. Fossils found in the rocks prove that climates have changed many times during the Earth's long history. In fact, the world is ever-changing as lands and seas very slowly alter position.

But natural land movements cannot explain all the changes. In the past 1.8 million years ice has covered much of North America and Europe several times. During the last Ice Age, the ice spread during cold periods and retreated during warm periods. Some scientists think changes in the tilt of the Earth's axis and its path round the Sun caused the last Ice Age, which ended around 10,000 years ago. But we may even be living in the warm period of a continuing Ice Age. Some day, perhaps, the ice will return.

Fossils help us to understand the climates of ancient times.

Air pollution

Today, many people think our weather is being changed by human activity. Factories have been powered by wood, coal, oil, and natural gas. They once poured smoke into the air, and many cities suffered from smog (a word made from two words: smoky fog). Most factories now use smokeless fuels, but industry still pours gases into the air, causing air pollution. Some gases are dissolved in water droplets, making acid rain that kills trees and a large number of the living creatures found in rivers and lakes.

Chemicals called CFCs have caused a serious problem. They are used in refrigerators and spray cans and have badly damaged parts of the ozone layer in the stratosphere. This allows more of the Sun's harmful ultraviolet rays to reach the ground.

Pollution belches from an oil drilling platform at sea.

In some cities, car exhausts cause severe smog.

Above *The burning of forests for agriculture causes major pollution—trees take carbon dioxide from the air, but forest fires actually create damaging carbon dioxide.*

Above *Vehicles are a major source of pollution.*

Clouds of moist air

Polluted air rises and mingles with moist clouds

Acid rain falls

Polluted rain soaks into the earth

Main sources of pollution in a developed area are general transport (50%), home heating (16%), industrial pollution (14%) and waste incineration (4%). Air pollution rises and mingles with water in the clouds to form destructive acid rain, and also returns to ground level where it adversely affects air quality for everyone.

28

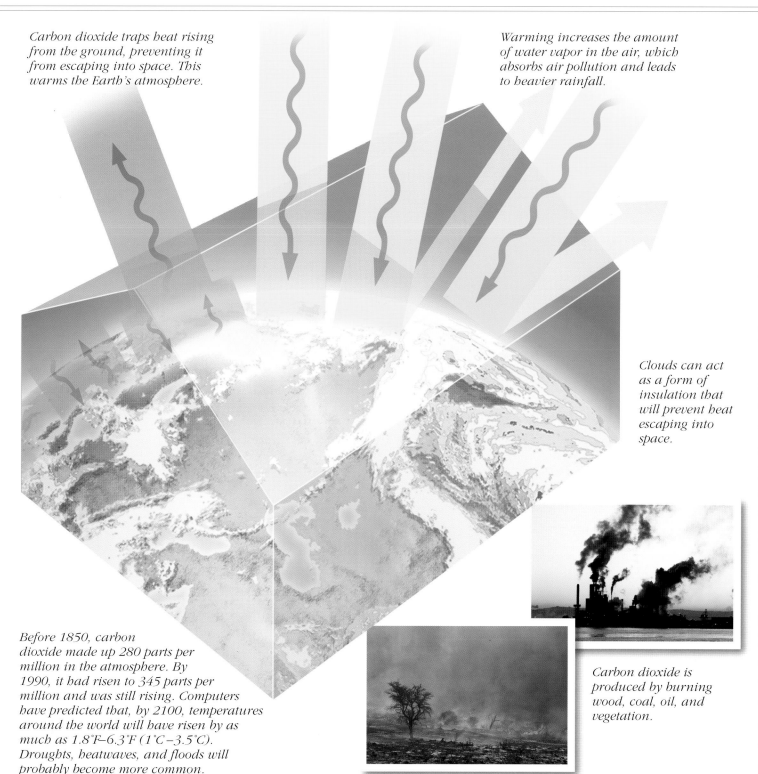

Carbon dioxide traps heat rising from the ground, preventing it from escaping into space. This warms the Earth's atmosphere.

Warming increases the amount of water vapor in the air, which absorbs air pollution and leads to heavier rainfall.

Clouds can act as a form of insulation that will prevent heat escaping into space.

Before 1850, carbon dioxide made up 280 parts per million in the atmosphere. By 1990, it had risen to 345 parts per million and was still rising. Computers have predicted that, by 2100, temperatures around the world will have risen by as much as 1.8°F–6.3°F (1°C–3.5°C). Droughts, heatwaves, and floods will probably become more common.

Global warming

Many scientists believe our planet is threatened by global warming, a term used to describe the over-heating of the Earth caused by pollution. A major factor in global warming is an increase of the amount of the gas carbon dioxide in the atmosphere.

Volcanoes also produce greenhouse gases.

Carbon dioxide is a greenhouse gas, along with methane and nitrous oxides (produced by factories and vehicles). Greenhouse gases act rather like the glass in a greenhouse. They let the Sun's heat pass through the atmosphere but prevent it all escaping back into space. As the volume of greenhouse gases in the atmosphere increases, so the temperature of the atmosphere will rise.

Global warming will affect everyone on Earth. Climates will change and sea levels will start to rise. Global warming will also have a great impact on our water, soils, plants, and animals.

Global warming will melt polar ice and raise sea levels. Some islands will then vanish.

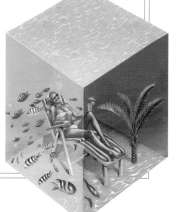

Carbon dioxide is produced by burning wood, coal, oil, and vegetation.

Weather records

Sun and rain

The driest place on Earth is the Atacama Desert in northern Chile. Years often go by with no rain, until a small freak storm occurs. By contrast, Cherrapunji, a village in northeastern India, had a record total rainfall of 1,041.77 in (26,461 mm) in just one year. The sunniest place in the world is claimed to be southwestern Arizona in the United States.

Left A scientist measures extremely low temperatures in Antarctica.

Left The coldest place on earth is the Antarctic. The sea ice never melts completely, even in the brief summer months.

Above The driest place on Earth is the Atacama Desert, Chile, South America.

Cold and hot

The coldest continent is Antarctica. The world's lowest temperature was recorded at Vostok, a Russian research station there. In 1983, a temperature of -89.2°F (128.6°C) was measured. The highest temperature, 136°F (58°C), was recorded at Al-Aziziyah, near Tripoli in Libya, North Africa.

Even camels feel the heat.

Above In California's Death Valley, the heat of the Sun evaporates any water, leaving salt behind.

Disasters

Floods can occur anywhere—even in some desert areas where flash floods briefly fill dry river beds. The world's worst flood took place in 1887, when the Huang He (Yellow River) burst its banks in China. Nearly a million people died. Bangladesh has regular floods. Some occur when winds drive the sea inland, others when the Brahmaputra, Ganges, and Meghna rivers are swollen by rainwater.

Floods often cause great damage.

Right In Bangladesh, people are used to dealing with monsoon conditions.

Winds

Right Mount Washington claims the honor of "the world's fastest gust".

The fastest-ever wind speed across the Earth's surface was recorded on the slopes of Mount Washington, in the United States. One gust of wind in April 1934 reached a speed of 231 mph (371 km/h). Gusts of wind that reach 220mph (354 km/h) often occur on Mount Washington. Strong winds can cause great damage, alone or in combination with other types of bad weather.

Below Hanging on for dear life!

Storms

Right Storms are a great hazard to shipping.

In 1988, a hurricane killed more than 350 people in the Caribbean, Mexico, and Texas. It made 750,000 people homeless and caused a massive amount of damage. In 1989, a tornado killed about 1,300 people in Bangladesh. In 1970, a million Bangladeshi people were killed by a tropical cyclone.

Left Global warming poses an increasing threat of flooding in coastal regions.

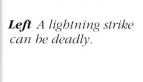

Left A lightning strike can be deadly.

Lightning

Lightning kills about 100 people a year in the United States alone. Lightning struck a former American park ranger named Roy C Sullivan seven times between 1942 and 1977. He suffered a variety of injuries and his hair was set alight—twice. But he was not killed by any of the strikes.

Right Soccer ball-sized hailstones have fallen in Asia.

Above A hailstorm with stones the size golf balls hit this main street in southern USA, where people know all about violent weather (*right*).

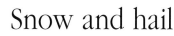

Snow and hail

Between February 19, 1971 and February 18, 1972, 1,224.5 in (31,102 mm) of snow fell at Paradise Ranger Station, Mount Rainier, in the US state of Washington. The largest known hailstones weighed up to 2 lb 3 oz (1 kg). They fell during a storm in Bangladesh in 1986. Reports stated that 92 people were killed.

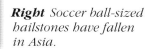

Index

acid rain 28
Africa 13, 20, 25
air 4, 9, 10, 13, 14, 15, 16, 18, 20, 23
air pollution 28
air pressure 4, 7, 13, 14, 18, 20, 21
aircraft 5, 22, 24
Al-Aziziyah 30
altocumulus 9
altostratus 9
anemometer 21
aneroid barometer 21
Antarctica 27, 30
anticyclone 14, 20, 23
Arctic 19
Arctic Ocean 27
argon 4
Arizona 30
Asia 13, 17, 20, 31
Atacama Desert 30
atmosphere, the 4, 5, 6, 7, 8, 22, 23, 25, 29
Australia 13, 17

balloons 5, 22
Bangladesh 30, 31
barograph 21
barometer, aneroid 21
blizzard 19
boulders 19
Brahmaputra River 30

California 30
carbon dioxide 4, 28, 29
Caribbean 17, 25, 31
cave drawings 27
caves 19
Central America 17
CFCs 28
charts 23, 24
Cherrapunji 13, 30
Chile 30
China 30
cholera 20
cirrocumulus 9
cirrostratus 9
cirrus 9
cities 19, 28
climate 3, 25, 26
climate changes 3, 27, 28
clouds 4, 9, 10, 11, 12, 15, 16, 17, 18, 22, 23, 28, 29
coal 28
cold and sunny climate 26
cold front 14, 15, 16, 23
cold temperatures 30
computers 23, 24, 29
condensation 9, 12, 16
convectional rainfall 10
crops 13, 21

cumulonimbus 9, 15, 16, 17, 18
cumulus 9, 17
cyclone 14, 17

Death Valley 30
depressions 14, 15, 23
deserts 7, 10, 19, 26, 27, 30
dew 9
dew point 9
Doldrums 7, 8
drought 20, 29
dry climates 26
dust 4, 19
duststorm 19

Earth, the 6, 7, 14, 22, 27, 29, 30
El Niño 27
Equator, the 5, 6, 7, 8, 10, 16, 17, 22, 25, 26
Europe 25, 27
evaporation 9, 10, 12
exosphere 5

factories 28, 29
fall 26
farmers 13, 21, 24
fir cones 21, 26
floods 8, 10, 13, 17, 20, 29, 30, 31

forecasts, forecasting 3, 21, 23, 24
forest fires 20, 28
forests 26, 27, 28
fossils 27
fronts 14, 15
frost 11, 21
funnels 18

Ganges River 30
glazed frost 11
global warming 29, 31
gravity 12
greenhouse gas 29
ground stations 22
Gulf Stream, the 25

hail 11, 21, 31
heat 20
heatwaves 20, 29
hoar frost 11
Honduras 20
horse latitudes 7, 8
Huang He (Yellow River) 30
humidity 20, 21, 22
hurricanes 17, 20, 31
hydrogen 22

ice 17, 19, 25, 26, 27, 30
Ice Age 27
ice crystals 4, 9, 10, 11

icestorms 19
India 30
industry 21, 28
isobars 14, 23

jet stream 5

Kilimanjaro 25

lakes 12, 28
land movement 27
latitude 7, 25
Libya 30
lightning 16, 31

malaria 20
maps 23, 24
Meghna River 30
mesosphere 5
meteorologists 21, 23, 24
meteorology 21
methane 29
Mexico 31
moisture 4, 5, 9, 10, 13
monsoon 13
mountains 10, 12, 25, 26
Mount Rainier 31
Mount Washington 31
mudslides 20

natural gas 28
New York 20

Nicaragua 20
nimbostratus 9
nitrogen 4
nitrous oxide 29
North Africa 30
North America 8, 17, 19, 26, 27
northern hemisphere 6, 7, 8, 15
North Pole 5, 6, 7

occluded front 14, 15, 23
ocean currents 25
oceans 12, 13, 17
oil 28
orographic rainfall 10
oxygen 4
ozone 5
ozone layer 5, 28

Pacific Ocean 27
photography, from space 22
plants 12, 13, 20, 25, 29
polar climates 26
polar easterlies 8
polar front 14
poles, the 5, 6, 7, 8, 14, 19, 22, 25
pollen 4
pollution, air 3, 28, 29
prairies 26

precipitation 11, 23
pressure 4, 7, 13, 14, 17, 18, 21
prevailing winds 8
prognostic charts 24

radar 22
radiation 5
radio-sondes 22
rain 10, 11, 12, 13, 15, 17, 20, 21, 22, 23, 25, 26, 29, 30
rainbow 10
raindrops 10
rainforest 26
rain gauge 21
rain shadow area 10
records 30
return stroke 16
rime 11
rivers 12, 20, 28, 30
Russia 19

salt 4, 30
sand 19
sandstorm 19
satellites 5, 22
savanna 26
sea 8, 10, 12, 13, 25, 27, 30
seasons 6, 26
Siberia 19

skin cancer 5
sleet 11
smog 28
snow 11, 12, 15, 19, 25, 26, 31
snowflake 11
soot 4
South America 30
southern hemisphere 6, 7, 8, 15
South Pole 5, 6, 7
space 5, 17, 22, 29
space shuttle 22
spring 13, 26
squall zone 18
storms 15, 17, 18, 20, 30, 31
stratocumulus 9
stratosphere 5, 22, 28
stratus 9
summer 6, 13, 16, 25, 26, 30
Sun 5, 6, 7, 10, 12, 20, 27, 28, 29, 30
sunshine recorder 21
Svalbard 27
synoptic charts 23, 24

Tanzania 25
temperate areas 7, 16, 19
temperate climate 26

temperatures 7, 13, 15, 20, 21, 22, 23, 25, 26, 29, 30
Texas 31
thermometer 21
thermosphere 5
thunder 16
thunderstorms 15, 16, 17
tornadoes 18, 31
tradewinds 8, 17, 27
transpiration 12
transport 21, 28
trees 12, 13, 18, 26, 28
Tripoli 30
tropical cyclones 17, 31
tropical rainy climate 26
tropopause 5
troposphere 5, 13, 22
tundra 26
twisters 18
typhoons 17

ultraviolet radiation 5, 28
United States 8, 13, 17, 18, 20, 30, 31

vegetation 25, 29
vehicles 19, 28, 29
volcanic ash 4
volcanoes 29
Vostok 30

warm front 14, 15, 23
Washington State 31
water cycle 12
water droplets 9, 10, 11, 17
waterspouts 18
water vapor 4, 9, 10, 12, 13, 15, 16, 20, 29
waves 17
weather center 23, 24
weather conditions 13, 21
weather forecasting 3, 21, 22, 23, 24
weather maps 14, 23, 24
weather stations 21, 23
weather warnings 3
westerly winds 8
willy-willies 17
wind 4, 8, 10, 12, 13, 14, 15, 17, 19, 25, 27, 30
wind speed 21, 23
wind vanes 21
winter 6, 8, 13, 25, 26
wood 28

Picture Credits

Maps: Mountain High Maps® Copyright©Digital Wisdom. *Icons:* Alex Charles. *Illustrations:* Julian Baker (JB Illustrations); Trevor Bounford; Sally Launder; Nicholas Rowland; John Woodcock. *Photographs:* Ancient Art & Architecture Collection Limited; British Antarctic Survey Photo Library; CASELLA CEL Limited, UK; Digital Vision; GeoScience Features Picture Library; International Weather Productions Ltd; National Meteorological Library and Archive, UK; National Oceanic and Atmospheric Administration/Department of Commerce, USA; Meteorological Office/Her Majesty's Stationery Office (London); Photodisc; Vaisala (UK) Limited. *Photographers:* Peter Dean (Frank Lane Picture Agency Limited); Kennith W. Fink (Ardea London); Francois Gohier (Ardea London); Jerry Mason (Science Photo Library); Sam Ogden (Science Photo Library); G. A. Robinson (National Meteorological Library and Archive).